nudes

a girl in love with
a boy in lust

for you.
for every piece of you
you've given away,
here's a piece back.

i hope it heals you.

note for the reader: the collection is chronology of events,
to see the chronology of emotions, follow the numbers.

tan tan, my angel, there aren't words enough in my head for the amount of thanks i owe to you. thank you for being my first reader, my constant encourager, my editor, for seeing the devices and praising my efforts. you listened without judgement and you hugged me when i needed you. most of all, thank you for driving me to realise my potential and being the best supporter and friend i could ever ask for – i am indebted to you.

r-patz, stevie, anna, bek, emily, chlo, keeley, felicity, alice; i owe you all the thanks in the world for taking the time to read my work and providing love, praise and support to make this the best it truly could be. you too are my editor; you made this possible.

all of you, and more, are the sisters that saved me. you're the sisters i rely on daily to warm me with your love. you are the sisters that i carry in my heart. you helped me heal, you kept me sane, you kept me on track. i praise the universe for bringing you to me.

sam

thank you for showing me the light when i could hardly see through the clouds. thank you for showing me my destiny in the cards.

i thank my lucky stars i found you and you lead me to this.

you are a savior.

love

three

109 nudes i told you i'd send by text one night.
here are those moments of complete vulnerability,
bare,
every ache and crevice of my body exposed.

sorry it took me so long,
i had to fall in love first

six

i'd never have let you
kiss me
if i knew every time our lips weren't
pressed together,
it would tear my heart
in two

five

i'm sorry, as we sat in your car,
two hand marks making a scarf around my throat,
the kiss still dancing on my lips,
i don't want to hurt you like that again you said as you
stared in my eyes.
shame, i breathed,
pain brings me alight

seventeen

on that night, where i laid in your arms,
salty tears rolling down my cheeks,
i spoke from honesty and truth.
you took my darkest secrets in your heart and freed me.
for that alone,
i could never forget you

seventy-nine

from the moment i'm awake, i can't wait for you to pick me up. to clock out of work, to run out those doors, to jump into your little red car spreads a grin across my face from ear to ear, knowing there is a kiss waiting for me inside, and a cuddle before you drive off awakens the butterflies within me and sets them off in a frenzy, knowing we will be talking nonsense on the drive, my hand resting on your leg, watching you gently command the steering wheel and divert your attention from the road to my eyes, and back, fills me with eternal joy.

you're the highlight of my day, every day. it's you

thirty-one

when you went to my room and read my poems,
i ripped my still beating heart right out of my chest
and placed it on a plate for you to examine
all it's scars

thirty-three

i feel myself clinging to you,
clutching for dear life, most days unable to let you go.
we lay in bed and i cannot bear to let the slightest of fabric
leave my fingertips.

i am scared

[one]

four

you fit in me like a puzzle piece;
comfy. cozy.
my nerves and fibres tingle and rejoice,
we are complete they cry

twenty

i think i'm falling in love with you
it took all my courage and might to admit this.
twenty-three years of building
defences,
walls,
armour.

in one sentence,
i tore it all down

sixty-four

every time you whisper
kiss me
into my ears,
it sends electricity down
my spine,
a current
through every vein
artery
muscle
bone
fragment
of my body.
it brings me alive;

a sensation that will never get old

seven

you kiss the delicate scarring of my inside thigh
and lick my swollen wounds,
until i cry with despair
i am free again

-grateful

thirty-four

i'm scared you will vanish. that tomorrow will be the day
you'll go;
you won't need me anymore.
there'll be another friend to caress and my
sweet nectar
will be honey
for a new bee.

you dislike my taste now, it serves you no purpose

[two]

eleven

after all this time,
to explore the great
beauties of the world
will complete me, but
leaving you behind is
sure to break my
heart

nineteen

we walked along the train platform,
arm in arm,
strolling home from a warm, summer day.
the air was hot,
we were floating from the alcohol,
activities,
excitement of us.
the moon illuminated your face as you said
i want to tell you something.
my body ached with anticipation for what was coming,

i'll never be prepared for the moment you told me
i'm falling in love with you too
no matter how many times
i relive it
in my
mind

twenty-nine

in your absence, i have begun cuddling the pillow
you lay your head on.
it's softer than your chest;
a roughness i have grown to miss

eighty-one

falling for you was the easiest thing i ever did,
as if it was made for me,
something i was meant to do,
it had been planned out for me my whole life.

and you, being you, made it so enjoyable

two

cradle me in your arms
Baby,
i'm forever yours

thirty-five

i'm scared i'll wake to an empty bed
with nothing but the delectable scent you leave behind
and the warmth your body once left on my sheets.

there'll be a gaping hole where you once were and i'll lay
there,

microscopic,

trying to fill the space

[three]

fifteen

with every touch
your fingertips imprinted on
me.
it's the most exquisite art i've
ever seen

forty-seven

i want to send you a photo of every
inch
of my body;
every curve, every line.
i don't.
honestly, i'm not sure whether it's because you still want
me,
or you know you can still have
me

ten

touch me tender,
love me tender,
and when i leave
make sure the knife
cuts me tender.
i can't bear for the scar to last forever

seventy-six

the very first time i tenderly ran my tongue over the curve of
your bottom lip, and you smiled, i felt a rush so hot, burning
with desire, bubbling with passion,
i chased that dragon.
every time i stroked my lips along your pelvis, breathing a
light, hot breath and your body tensed along with your
giggle,
i chased that dragon.
every time you were curved over me, bodies as one, a bead
of god-knows-whose sweat trickling down between my
breasts,
i chased that dragon.
every time you stroked my hair with one hand, the other
caressing my thigh, my side, my stomach; your lips
caressing mine,
i chased that dragon.
you are my drug. i'm so addicted, i think it might
kill me

eighteen

they say
love is blindness,
but i'd never seen such beauty before my time with you;
Baby
if that's blindness then have my eyes
forever

eight

every time you smile at a message, sender unknown,
i tear a chunk from my body.

with each photo received of a face unrecognised,
a fairer hair,
chocolatey eyes
or velvet skin,
i rip another piece of me.

when you embrace another woman whose being doesn't
curve the way mine does into yours,
i drain blood from my veins.

Baby, when i'm kneeling in front of you,
bleeding,
in tatters,
then will you love only me?

-paranoia

eighty-two

make love to me
i whisper in your ear
and the world changes.
the rhythm, the touch,
the feel, the emotion.
everything is different.
i've never felt that before.
it is a crescendo of excitement,
desire, intensity, love.
better than any time
we've spent together.
better than any time i think
i'll spend with anyone else.
when you make love to me,
it's as though every dream i ever had
came true, all at once

sixty-six

you curled into me, cradling my quivering body,
tears rolling down my cheeks whilst my stomach burned
with a pain
far greater than you'll ever know.
marie had a light touch and was so understanding, but i hope
to god,
the universe,
that i never have to see her again.
i cried myself to sleep that night,
through the pain, in your embrace,
like your baby.

it was both the best and worst thing i've done.
to have had a part of you with me,
forever,
would have been the most bittersweet of
endings

thirty-six

i'm scared you no longer find me interesting
or intriguing
or exciting.

i am of no use to you anymore

[four]

sixty-eight

there's a twinkling star in the sky.
the brightest and most beautiful one,
and when the lights are out,
and the world is still,
it glistens under the blanket of white bursts and supernovas.
it's a part of us both;
half of you,
half of me.
i've been waking up a lot in the night,
reason unknown,
just to fall back asleep moments later.
it's waking me up to say
i was here, i still am.
don't forget me

thirty-eight

everything in my bed smells like you.
as i lay entangled, it seeps deep into me
like the sweetest perfume
sprayed over my delicate skin.

i bathe in the scent,
missing every moment.
and every time, even when you aren't here,
the smell brings you back
to my arms

thirty

each time you tell me
i won't be staying at yours again,
i am smug. i'm taking wagers;
you'll be back in my bed in a week and once again
i'll be the winner

eighty

no man has ever done me
like you do.
no man has ever thought of me
like you do.
no man has ever put my pleasure before his
like you do.
no man has ever got me there
like you do.
no man has ever kissed me
like you do.

maybe this is why i refuse to
let you go

forty-nine

i left part of myself behind when i left you.
now i'm chasing after you breathlessly,
screaming
wait! i need you back

forty-six

every step i have taken on this trip,
i've taken holding your hand

seventy-seven

the bruise is long gone.
the pain, disappeared.
the red print has vanished.
but there on my behind remains a branding.
your hand is scarred into my skin.
to remind the next one.
and the one after that.
and the one after that.
even when i'm his
i'm forever yours

forty-four

every night i have been away from you,
from across the world,
the thought of you cradles me
to sleep

thirty-seven

but most of all,
i am scared
to lose
love

[five]

one

we were swept up in the hurricane of it all
and in it we lost our inhibitions,
the only thing there to remind us the reality

we aren't meant to be.

after love

twenty-two

you told me you were just like the others.
Baby
it never occurred to me for one second
you were telling the truth

sixty-nine

he loves me.
he loves me not.
he wants me.
he wants me not.
he needs me.
he needs me not.
he has me.
he has me not.
he misses me.
he misses me not.
he cares for me.
he doesn't give a shit.

-
why do we torture ourselves?

thirteen

i left part of myself behind when i followed you.
tonight, i'm breathlessly chasing after her,
screaming
wait! i need you back

thirty-nine

there was no need to make me
hate you
just because you wanted to
feel better
about missing me

i hope you hate yourself
too

eighty-four

am i actually pretty
was i boring
did i satisfy you
how long did it go on for
why her and not me
wasn't i enough

                all the answers i'll never know

did you really love me?

              the only one i care about

fourteen

those ghosts clawed at my trust
until every fragment was gone.
they whisper in my ear when you aren't around.
because of them, every time i see you with her
my heart tears a little bit more

seventy-one

you could have told me the earth was square
dogs can't look up
you loved me
and i would have believed every single word
as gospel

-influence

sixteen

with every touch
your fingers imprinted on
me.
i want to tear the painting apart,
removing all evidence that the art
ever existed

forty-two

i used to appreciate our time together.
now i wish i'd
never
fucking
met
you,
Baby

nine

you made me hate my sisters,
living in fear of their existence.
did you know they'd one day be my allies
in the fight for your love,
or my sanity?

forty

the night you called her
the one, my heart broke
into a thousand pieces.
one day a real man will
piece it back together
and uncover the
devastation you left
behind

seventy-two

if you followed your mind
as much as you follow your dick,
you'd be unstoppable

fifty-six

i was clay;
you moulded me,
shaped and positioned me,
tied and bound me,
created the image you wanted to see.

i was a monet;
you observed me,
stared and questioned me,
criticised and discussed me,
decided i wasn't an image you wanted to keep.

i was a mannequin;
you controlled me,
removed and unpeeled me,
moved and positioned me,
dressed me the way you wanted to be.

it was so subtle i never realised i lost my
identity

-manipulation

sixty

i tried to make myself prettier, to be
less like the others.
for what? i was a target board
just like the others,
to practice on.

i hope that old board you went back to
suits your needs better, the rest of us grew
tired
of having holes darted into us

fifty-five

i was always staring at you in the car,
when you hated it,
when you asked me to stop,
when you asked me *why?*
because i was searching for their faces in yours

that was a convincing camouflage

-clarification

fifty-nine

you told me i had no worth.
who the fuck do you think i am?

Baby, you were lucky to have ever touched me

seventy-four

it's okay, the wetter the better.
funny how you
changed your tune
when it was
coming from my
eyes and not
my pants

twenty-six

i know peace is within me, i have felt it before.
but it's hard to find when you've extinguished
my only flame

forty-three

over the course of your blossoming *friendship* my heart was
exhausting itself
every day,
to push the blood around my body as it wept at the
loss of your embrace.
it endured its first slow and painful devastation; one i fear it
will never recover from.

i couldn't eat.
sleep became a thing i neglected, as i searched messages
and memories for some spec of confirmation that really
you did love me.
in this quest i found nothing but
pain and disappointment,
and the fibres of my heart screamed in sorrow every time.
then you called her *the one*.
in those two words, you punched your
closed fist into my chest,
clutching my crying, aching heart;
veins bursting between your fingers,
beating against your palm,
and you gently pulled it away from its home.
so gently that every fibre that tore, every vein that ripped
was felt in all its devastation;

i could never forget that pain. i stood there
breathless, cold and numb.
it was never broken, you took it from me
and now because of you, i fear i'll live without a heart
for the rest of my life.

i kept this for so long that it's eaten at the rest of my organs
like a virus;
a plague.
now my power is in my truth and i'm going to teach the
world to love in a way that you
never could

fifty-four

i once carried around a bag so heavy,
so full of dead weight,
dead emotion and memories,
it brought me to my knees every day.
then i met you and it
felt like
you were removing those dead weights
slowly every day.
it took me eight months, a plane trip around the world
and peace
to realise you were just replacing
my old with your new,
dead emotions and memories
slowly every day

sixty-seven

i much prefer your tongue
when it's not talking

forty-five

i spend every day in between
the then,
and the now.
blissfully living in the memory of you
holding me
between the sheets

sixty-three

you two are so good together.
they were right, we were.

too bad you fucked it

twenty-seven

what use is faith in the future,
if you don't have the positivity it will
come?

seventy

you used to tell me i wanted too much sex.
why?

it was the easiest way to shut you up.
it worked every time

sixty-one

my only regret was allowing you
to convince me
we didn't need protection.

realistically, i needed protection from you;
the one thing you could never do

-irony

seventy-eight

my skin itches. i am tearing at it with my nails. clawing at
the irritation under my skin. the things i want to say, the
things i know i can't say, the things i'm too scared to say.
my sisters watch on in silence; they are making sure i don't
message you.

i'm scratching *bless you* into my skin

forty-one

i really thought i would love you
forever.
now i can't imagine a second passing by
where i feel anything
for you

seventy-five

remember that time i pinned you down,
wrists tied above your head
to my bed,
eyes lightly covered with your blindfold,
mouth held open unable to speak,
naked,
senseless on my bed,
my tongue delicately exploring your body.

tell me, did you enjoy finally being
powerless?

fifty-seven

you are the man of my dreams.
unfortunately for you

my dreams have changed

seventy-three

i sent this collection,
the nudes, to you.
you responded
i didn't see any nudes.

here it is. i know it's an old one
but you don't deserve to see how
beautiful this process has made
me now

twenty-one

some we share, i never wish to remember.
some we share, i never wish to forget.
some are mentioned daily and break my heart every time.
some i want to declare from the rooftops.
our moment was my fate,
written in the stars,
and will forever be part of my soul;

even when i am only a memory people hold.

-moments

healing

twenty-three

i can see why they loved you.
you're a miracle, a prayer.

                              a godsend.
you worshipped my flaws,
you took my inner hatred and you taught me to love.
i imagine you did this for us all;

                              we smile because of you,
you freed us.
you showed us what to expect, what to command, what to
desire.
the rest will be easy because you did what you came to do
and taught us how to love and live
after love is lost.
but baby, when you are teaching women
to be women,

            to love who they truly are,
please remember to love yourself.
allow yourself to find love again,
this isn't all you are destined for.
don't waste your treasure on

                              a lonely life.
don't fear what the next one will do to you
whilst you are lifting her up.

baby, you deserve all the pieces of you
that you give to every girl

                              back.
there will be a love out there for you that is truly
magical.
as magical as you made us

twelve

you taught me my strength
and now
my superpower
is your
kryptonite

twenty-four

we'll never know what the future holds
for us.
all i've come to learn is this:
timing truly is everything

sixty-five

now all is said and done,
i finally recognise your purpose.
you took all my demons when i offered them,
and together we let them go.

-thank you

twenty-eight

i am Woman.

our mothers fought for the freedom i exercise.

i am Woman.

no longer will man command me.

i am Woman.

power is in my emotion.

i am Woman.

my worth is dictated by me and no other.

i am Woman.

my roar, like lion, will halt you.

i am Woman.

to be nasty, free, us, is pure magic.

i am Woman.

it is my obligation to fight, hand in hand with my Sisters til
our knuckles bleed, head bowed, kneeling at the finish line.

i am Woman.

with a dirty mouth i scream

fuck you

forty-eight

sometimes, even those allies can be enemies
in disguise.
be grateful for them,
they teach you the biggest
lessons

thirty-two

allowing you to experience me is a privilege,
not a shame.
i am not a trophy;
remember that as you slander my name

fifty

i saw a cute couple on the beach today.
he kissed her so passionately on the cheek,
i smiled at the love between them.
i knew then that you couldn't give me all i wanted
because that's not you.
in that instant,
i let your memory float out to sea

twenty-five

to my greatest love; my Sisters,
let me teach you a beautiful lesson.
when you are laying in the ashes,
smoke billowing from the ground,
burnt and bruised and willing to give in,
remember one thing:

rise to your weary feet,
war paint your face with ash
and march on with fire on your tail.
our fight never ends, we only gain

perspective

fifty-one

i regret every occasion i took
my own time
to send you a fragment of me.

with every photo, every video, every word,
i fell deeper
into a hole i could never claw my way out of.

it took the little courage
i had left
to see you write *it's never gonna happen.*

but without a
pang of regret
i let you go

fifty-eight

you were a trophy.
like the metal,
your skin is cold and tarnished
by the touch of someone who cared only to own you
and not keep you.
like the shape,
your curves are subtle and smooth,
once appreciated for a moment
before the novelty wore off and your appeal was lost.
like the handles,
you were gripped and groped,
held down and ruthlessly paraded around;
a temporary pride.
like the name placard,
your purpose, your identity is unimportant.
it is your appearance, the accolade,
that is celebrated.
i too was a trophy.
but Sister, even after we're discarded
and the next one has grasped us by the handles
and is gripping us to their chest,
rest assured:
we are the real winners
all the time the ones who held us down
are the losers of our past

sixty-two

you could do better.
maybe, but i don't want to.

sometimes you just owe it to yourself

fifty-two

it never felt so good to be rid.
i taste the sweet nectar of freedom,
opportunity
                adventure
                    real love

dancing on my lips, dribbling down my chin and dripping
onto my chest.
the empty cavity warms to the feeling of this honey,
knowing
soon my heart will grow there again, it will
burst with the sweet, delicious nectar,
you could never really give me. i will love.

and letting go was
the best thing
i
could ever do

fifty-three

with everything you do,
always remember the incentive is

for the love of me

-reminder

eighty-three

Sister, if you invested half the courage it took to
confess your love
into building yourself,
you'd be a force
unstoppable.

so would you rather be their shadow,
or your own light?

eighty-five

all those unanswered questions
i had,
i found the truth here:

do i really love me?
yes love, you do.

one last reminder: no matter how horrible the pain, love will always be worth it.

Printed in Great Britain
by Amazon